Titles of the
Holy Spirit

D0813807

TITLES OF THE HOLY SPIRIT

A manual for prayer and praise based on titles of the Holy Spirit

Keith A. Fournier

Franciscan University Press
Steubenville, Ohio

Cover: Photograph of a stained glass window in San Marco Catholic Church, Marco Island, Florida

> *Window Design:* Kate White Shulok, White Stained Glass Studio, Inc., Sarasota, Florida

> *Photography:* John Cress
> Cress Photography,
> Sarasota, Florida

Cover Design: Art Mancuso

Inside Graphics: Colleen Johnson

Copyright © 1989 Franciscan University Press, All rights reserved

Available from: Franciscan University Press
Franciscan University of
Steubenville
Steubenville, OH 43952

Printed in the United States of America

ISBN 0-940535-21-1

DEDICATION

This book is lovingly and admiringly dedicated to three Apostles of the Holy Spirit:

His Holiness, Pope John XXIII whose courage and leadership opened the windows of the Church to a new wave of the Holy Spirit;

The Reverend David DuPlessis, ''Mr. Pentecost,'' whose pentecostal passion for the things of God, whose conviction that ''God has no grandchildren'' and whose love for all followers of Jesus paved the way for much of the current ecumenical cooperation accompanying the Spirit's work in our day;

And finally, to my dear friend and brother, Reverend Harald Bredesen, ''Mr. Charisma,'' who seems to have inherited the mantle of his pentecostal predecessor and who, standing on the courage of his convictions and led always by his trusted advisor, the Holy Spirit, is not afraid to champion new horizons.

TABLE OF CONTENTS

PART I
Titles of the Holy Spirit

PART II
Prayers to the Holy Spirit

INTRODUCTION

This devotional book came to me as a fruit of prayer, the best place for such a book to find its beginning. I had been deeply moved by **Titles of Jesus** written by my friend, Father Michael Scanlan. My relationship with the Lord and my love for Him have grown deeper as a result of my reflecting on the titles of Jesus.

During my family vacation one summer, I began to reflect on the Holy Spirit who also is a divine person of the Blessed Trinity. I began to search the Sacred Scriptures for the names and titles of the Holy Spirit. As I did, I found the same treasure, a new relationship with God the Holy Spirit.

Throughout the ages, prophets predicted that the day would come when God would give his Spirit freely to men.

> In the last days, God says,
> I will pour out my Spirit on all people.
>
> Your sons and daughters will prophesy,
> your young men will see visions,
> your old men will dream dreams.
>
> Even on my servants, both men and women,
> I will pour out my Spirit in those days,
> and they will prophesy.

I will show wonders in the heaven above
and signs on the earth below,
blood and fire and billows of smoke.

The sun will be turned to darkness
and the moon to blood
before the coming of the great and
  glorious day of the Lord.

And everyone who calls
on the name of the Lord will be saved.
(Joel 2:17-21)

Those who turned to Him and received
His spirit would be transformed:

I shall give you a new heart, and put a new
spirit in you; I shall remove the heart of
stone from your bodies and give you a
heart of flesh instead. I shall put my spirit
in you. (Ezekiel 36:22-28)

Moreover, Jesus promised before He
died that He would give His followers the
Holy Spirit, and this promise is for all of
us.

If you love me you will keep my commandments. I shall ask the Father, and he
will give you another Advocate to be with
you forever, that Spirit of truth whom the
world can never receive because it neither
sees nor knows him; but you know him
because he is with you. (John 14:15-18)

On the day of Pentecost, the disciples,
together with the mother of Jesus, were

gathered together in one room in prayer. The Holy Spirit came upon them fulfilling the prophecy of Joel. As they began to experience the living power of God, a once frightened assemblage began teaching and boldly preaching the message of salvation. The Church was born at Pentecost and accomplished the monumental task of spreading the gospel throughout the first-century world through the gifts of the Spirit. We must realize that these gifts are not only for the apostles; the gifts of the Spirit continue to build the church. Are we not all called to build the church of Christ? You can experience the Holy Spirit the same way the first disciples did. Whether you have been a Christian for some time or have never believed in Christ, you can receive the Spirit afresh, in a moment. All it takes is an invitation. The Holy Spirit continues to come in a continual process of transformation.

When the Spirit is released within you, you will not only know God as a deep reality in your life, but you will also experience a transformation that will become obvious in the fruits of your actions. In addition to this means of personal change, God gives the Holy Spirit so that we, as the body of Christ, can be united more fully. As Christians, we all have different functions, but we are one in the same Spirit (Ephesians 4:4).

Praying to the Holy Spirit is a long standing tradition in the church, but is somewhat less common in the experience of the faithful. We all know about the suffering, death, and resurrection of Jesus. As Catholics we know that at Mass, we enter into the timeless sacrifice of Christ to the Father. However, we often neglect to embrace the power of the Holy Spirit in our lives. We can and should pray for the presence of the Holy Spirit on a daily basis.

One of the most beautiful and powerful forms of prayer to the Holy Spirit is the Novena to the Holy Spirit, a tradition which is tied directly to the time of Christ. Jesus told His apostles in Jerusalem to await the coming of the Holy Spirit, the first Pentecost:

> You are witnesses of this. See, I send down upon you the promise of my Father. Remain here in the city until you are clothed with power from on high.
> (Luke 24:48:49 NAB)

Christian tradition has always held that the apostles waited for nine days. Therefore, the first ''novena'' was one which invoked the Holy Spirit. This novena is the only one recorded in scripture and is still strongly encouraged by the Church. Addressed to the third person of the Trinity, it is powerful plea for guidance through the operation of the seven gifts of the Holy Spirit — wisdom, understanding, counsel, fortitude, knowledge, piety, and fear of the Lord.

While the novena is a wonderful structured guide for prayer, it is only one form of devotion. There are many other ways to invoke the Holy Spirit in prayer. The easiest way is simply to ask God for His gift. But, before you pray, always remember that God loves you and desires that you have the fullness of life that He promised. And this fullness of life is experienced by following the movement of the Spirit in your life.

God desires renewal in each heart and renewal in the Church. Let us work together in unity with the Holy Spirit to renew the face of the earth. The following prayer spoken by Pope John XXIII is a powerful model of how and why we invoke the Holy Spirit of God:

Renew Your wonders in this our day, as by a new Pentecost. Grant to Your Church that, being of one mind and steadfast in prayer with Mary, the Mother of Jesus, and following the lead of blessed Peter, it may advance the reign of our Divine Savior, the reign of truth and justice, the reign of love and peace. Amen.

The role of the Holy Spirit, as defined clearly by the Second Vatican Council, is to sanctify the Church so that those who believe might have access through Christ in one Spirit to the Father.

> The Spirit dwells in the Church and in the hearts of the faithful...renews her and leads her to perfect union with her spouse.
> (Lumen Gentium, art. 4)

Pope John XXIII initiated a renewed interest in the Holy Spirit. The council fathers completed this work in order to foster strong devotion to the Spirit of God. The Church realizes that Her mission is only accomplished in and through the power of the Spirit.

Although the Catholic Church has always recognized the need for the Spirit, in the last twenty-five years the emphasis has been heightened. In particular the charismatic renewal and dialogue with our Pentecostal brothers and sisters have increased our awareness and understanding of the tremendous outpouring of the Holy Spirit in our times.

This devotional book is meant to be used as a manual much like Father Michael's **Titles of Jesus.** It is not so much to be read as to be prayed, silently or vocally. I have not used the great wealth of other titles given to the Spirit by the Church over the centuries but have confined the choice of titles to the scriptural text.

A helpful tool for prayer to the Holy Spirit is to discover and meditate on who He is. Here is where this book can be instrumental. These various titles of the Holy Spirit are meant to be a beginning, a tool for coming to a greater awareness of God in your life, a tool that must be built upon by your personal reflection and response.

The second part of the book contains traditional prayers to the Holy Spirit.

HOW TO USE
THE MANUAL

How should you use the manual? Use it in the way that most helps you to pray. Here are some suggestions:

1) Familiarize yourself with the titles and repeat them daily in your prayer.

2) Develop one title each day as a point of prayer. Ask the Holy Spirit to reveal to you the depth of meaning of the title. Look up the full scripture passages.

3) Select a rotation of the titles to deepen your appreciation for each one.

4) Memorize the titles using the alphabetic order to fix them in your mind and frequently, at least daily, use them in praise.

PART I
TITLES OF THE HOLY SPIRIT

COUNSELOR

Scripture: John 14:16
And I will ask the Father, and He will give you another Counselor to be with you forever - the Spirit of truth.

Reflection: I am no longer alone. I have as my confidant and trusted advisor, the very Spirit of God. The Spirit which searches my heart reveals His mind, and has the assigned task of leading me into all truth (Romans 8:27). In our age many seek after counselors to clear out the confusion of the contemporary age. Many of those are false counselors leading the way to death and destruction. The Holy Spirit is a true counselor who leads those submitted to his direction to the truth of God's word found in His scriptures and His church. The Holy Spirit is a counselor and a confidant to be trusted, sought out and followed.

Prayer: Lord Jesus, your prayers are always heard by the eternal Father. You petitioned that the Counselor be sent and He has come. Open my ears to hear His advice; soften my heart to be formed by it and direct my paths toward truth.

Decision: Today, I will seek as my first Counselor, the Holy Spirit.

Petition: Come, Holy Spirit...

HOLY SPIRIT

Scripture: Psalm 51:11, Ephesians 1:13-14,
Ephesians 4:30
*Do not cast me from your presence or take
your Holy Spirit from me.*

*And you also were included in Christ when
you heard the word of truth, the gospel of
your salvation. Having believed, you were
marked in him with a seal, the promised
Holy Spirit, who is a deposit guaranteeing
our inheritance until the redemption of
those who are God's possession - to the
praise of his glory.*

*And do not grieve the Holy Spirit of God,
with whom you were sealed for the day of
redemption.*

Reflection: God is all Holy. In Him there
is no taint of sin and no darkness
(1 John 1:5). I am not holy. Yet through
His great love and the mystery of
grace, I am being made new (2 Corinthians 5:17), recreated into the image
of the Holy. All that is of the ''former
manner of life'' is being purified so that
I can decrease and He can increase.
This is a gift which requires my
response of consecration, being set

apart (Galatians 1:15) so that I too can become holy through His holiness at work within me.

Prayer: Holy Spirit, purify me by the power of your love and burn away all manner of evil, sin and vice. Make me a consecrated vessel and seal me unto the day of redemption.

Decision: Today I will consecrate my life to the Holy Spirit and allow Him to purify me.

Petition: Come, Holy Spirit...

POWER OF THE MOST HIGH

Scripture: Luke 1:35
The angel answered, 'The Holy Spirit will come upon you, and the power of the Most High will overshadow you. So the holy one to be born will be called the Son of God.'

Reflection: The Power of God overshadowed the Blessed Virgin of Nazareth and through her fiat and the Spirit's power she became the Ark of the New Covenant, the dwelling place of the Saviour. That same power will overshadow all of those who acknowledge their littleness before the Father and obey His Word. They, today, can become tabernacles of the Most High, with Jesus Christ living within them, continuing His redemptive work through His church.

Prayer: Almighty and all-powerful God overshadow me with your power that Christ may be formed in me and I can become a vessel of honor (2 Timothy 2:20-21) and an instrument of your eternal plan.

Decision: Today I will follow the example of Mary, the first disciple, and allow myself to be overshadowed by the Holy Spirit, the power of the Most High.

Petition: Come, Holy Spirit...

SPIRIT OF ADOPTION

Scripture: Romans 8:15 (NAB)

You did not receive a spirit of slavery leading you back into fear, but a spirit of adoption through which we cry out, "Abba!" (that is, "Father").

Reflection: "Fear is useless, what is needed is trust" (Mark 5:36b NAB). We have received the Spirit of Adoption and by it we have been incorporated into the very family of God. No longer are we alone. We have the God of the whole universe as "Abba" and by grace we have been grafted into His Vine (Romans 11:1-22), His family. The implications of this are overwhelming. Our status, our destiny, our inheritance, and our very position became transformed. The decree of adoption was signed in the blood of the "First-born among many brothers..." (Romans 8:29), Jesus, the "faithful Witness" (Revelation 3:14), and sealed by the Spirit, the pledge of our inheritance (Ephesians 1:13-14).

Prayer: Father, help me this day to live in the reality of my adoption as your son/daughter and no longer fear any circumstance which would rob me of my status in the family.

Decision: Today I will live as a son/daughter of God in the full inheritance and provision of Jesus Christ by the Spirit of Adoption.

Petition: Come, Holy Spirit...

SPIRIT OF CHRIST

Scripture: 1 Peter 1:10-11

Concerning this salvation, the prophets, who spoke of the grace that was to come to you, searched intently and with the greatest care, trying to find out the time and circumstances to which the Spirit of Christ in them was pointing when he predicted the sufferings of Christ and the glories that would follow.

Reflection: ''The Christ,'' the anointed one. The Prophets longed to see His day and foretold of His mighty deliverance from bondage; His passion, suffering and humiliation; His death and resurrection (Matthew 26-28; Mark 14-16; Luke 22-24; John 18-21). That Spirit of anointing still points toward the final consummation when He will return to subject all things to Himself and deliver the Kingdom to the Father. To those who live in Him (Act 17:28), the Spirit of Christ points toward the final promised redemption when the fullness of God's eternal promises and provision will be revealed, when his sons and daughters will be clothed in immortality (1 Corinthians 15:54) and creation itself redeemed (Romans 8:23).

Prayer: Lord Jesus Christ, may the Spirit of prophetic anointing well up within me enabling me to live my life by faith with an eternal perspective, longing for your second coming.

Decision: Today I will call on the Spirit of Christ to direct my thoughts, words and actions that I might become a prophetic sign pointing toward the second coming.

Petition: Come, Holy Spirit...

SPIRIT OF COUNSEL

Scripture: Isaiah 11:2
> *The Spirit of the Lord will rest on him - the Spirit of wisdom and of understanding, the Spirit of counsel and of power, the Spirit of knowledge and of the fear of the Lord.*

Reflection: The Holy Spirit spoke through the prophet Isaiah and heralded the coming of Christ. The Spirit of Counsel would rest upon Him. The Holy Spirit is a counselor, who gives advice and direction to those who ask. This counsel leads to power and knowledge and is the fruit of the life dedicated to fear of the Lord.

Prayer: Lord Jesus Christ, you are that righteous Branch promised through the Prophet. The Holy Spirit rests upon you and those who join you through your body, the Church. Fill me with your Spirit of Counsel that I may grow in the knowledge and fear of the Lord.

Decision: Today I will seek Godly counsel and rely less on my own human wisdom. Today I will seek a direction from the Holy Spirit of Good Counsel.

Petition: Come, Holy Spirit...

SPIRIT OF THE FATHER

Scripture: Matthew 10:19-20

But when they arrest you, do not worry about what to say or how to say it. At that time you will be given what to say, for it will not be you speaking, but the Spirit of your Father speaking through you.

Reflection: Jesus taught us to call God our Father and then through His great act of love cleared the way for our restoration and participation in His very intimate walk with the Father. Through the Spirit, we now have the very life of God within us. It is the Spirit, Jesus tells us, who will give us the very words of the Father in the day of trouble. It is the same Spirit who spoke through the clouds on the day of Jesus' baptism by the Jordan River and proclaimed, ''This is my beloved Son'' (Mark 1:11). We too are beloved sons and daughters and now His Father is our Father (John 20:17).

Prayer: Father, fill me with your Spirit in the day of trial and every day so that I may be faithful to the mission you have entrusted to me.

Decision: Today, I will walk as a son/
daughter, confident of my relationship
with a loving Father who will provide
for me in the midst of struggle.

Petition: Come, Holy Spirit...

SPIRIT OF FIRE

Scripture: Hebrews 12:29, Luke 3:16
Our God is a consuming fire.

He will baptize you with the Holy Spirit and with fire.

Reflection: Fire burns. It purifies metal and consumes wood. The Lord wants our lives to be built on rock and he sends the Spirit of the refiner's fire to consume all in our life that is not leading us closer to Him. We need to let that fire fall freely upon us so that it may do its work.

Prayer: Come Spirit of Fire and consume me, purify me, melt away the hardness of my heart. Baptize me so that what is left when you are done with your work is the very image of Jesus Christ.

Decision: Today I will see all difficulty and trial which God does not take away as an occasion for refining and a sign of the Spirit of Fire at work within me.

Petition: Come, Holy Spirit...

SPIRIT OF GLORY

Scripture: 1 Peter 4:14

If you are insulted because of the name of Christ, you are blessed, for the Spirit of glory and of God rests on you.

Reflection: The glory of God settled on Mount Sinai (Exodus 2:16) and God gave to His servant Moses His plan for His people. The Spirit of Glory followed God's people in a pillar and a cloud during their sojourn through the desert. The Spirit of glory so transformed Moses that His face radiated (Exodus 34-29). The Spirit of Glory rested fully on and flowed from the divine Son of God, Jesus Christ, on the mountain of transfiguration (Luke 9:32) and at the moment of his resurrection. When He comes again it will be in a cloud, with great power and great glory (Luke 21:27). Jesus prayed, in His high priestly prayer (John 17), that the same Spirit of Glory would come upon his followers. The apostle Peter tells us that glory is given to us most when we suffer with the Lord and so share in His cross (1 Peter 4:14).

Prayer: Father, send your Spirit of Glory upon me that I may deem it a privilege and an honor to suffer for the name of Christ. Let that Spirit consume all within me which would fight to protect myself rather than fight to honor your name.

Decision: Today I will accept all suffering and struggle which isn't removed through prayer and right living as an occasion of grace, relying on the Spirit of Glory.

Petition: Come, Holy Spirit...

SPIRIT OF GOD

Scripture: Genesis 1:2
Now the earth was formless and empty, darkness was over the surface of the deep, and the Spirit of God was hovering over the waters.

Reflection: From the beginning the presence of the Spirit of God hovered over the waters. The Holy Spirit still "hovers" over the earth drawing men and women and indeed all of creation (Romans 8:22) into the full redemption God desires. It is by the Spirit of God that we are recreated into the image of Christ (2 Corinthians 5:17).

Prayer: God the Father, by your Spirit and through your Son the earth was created and is recreated. Life is breathed into mankind. By that same Spirit move in me that I may be recreated, leaving behind the formless and empty deeds of the flesh in order to embrace fully your plan for my life.

Decision: Today, I will open my whole life to the Spirit of God so that I may be recreated into the image of Christ.

Petition: Come, Holy Spirit. . .

SPIRIT OF GRACE AND SUPPLICATION

Scripture: Zechariah 12:10
And I will pour out on the house of David and the inhabitants of Jerusalem a spirit of grace and supplication.

Reflection: The promise given through the prophet was that the Spirit of humble prayer would be given to God's chosen people. Hundreds of years later a Virgin named Mary was visited by an angel who proclaimed to her, "Hail, full of grace, the Lord is with you" (Luke 1:28 ff). Through her co-operation with that Spirit of Grace, her "Fiat" (Luke 1:46 ff), her "yes," the God of the Universe took on flesh and was born among us.

Prayer: Father, send that same Spirit of Grace and Supplication which over-shadowed Mary to us today and by it strengthen our resolve to bring the message of your Son Jesus Christ into the midst of a needy world. Give me that Spirit of Grace and Supplication that I might join my "yes" with that of countless millions who through the ages have become disciples of your Son and workers in your vineyard.

Decision: Today, I will say my "yes" by word and deed to the Lord's call and so co-operate with the Spirit of Grace and Supplication.

Petition: Come, Holy Spirit...

SPIRIT OF HOLINESS

Scripture: Romans 1:3-4

> *. . . regarding His Son, who as to His human nature was a descendant of David, . . . and who through the Spirit of Holiness was declared with power to be the Son of God by His resurrection from the dead: Jesus Christ our Lord.*

Reflection: The Spirit of Holiness declared the sonship of Jesus in his triumph over death and through His Holy Life. That same Holy Spirit works in the believer and we are called to be holy (1 Thesessalonians 4:3 ff). We are called to manifest the holiness of Jesus Christ. It is the Spirit of God which perfects us. The Greek word, found in the admonition of Jesus, ''Be perfect as I am perfect'' (Matthew 5:48), is ''Teleios'' and it refers to our accomplishing what we were created to be. Those of us who belong to Christ have been recreated to be like Him and it is the Spirit of Holiness which will bring that about.

Prayer: Father, send the Spirit of Holiness upon me that I too may find my sonship and identity in being conformed to the all holy image of your beloved Son, Jesus Christ.

Decision: This day I will take holiness seriously, and as much as it depends on me, cooperate with the Spirit of Holiness at work within me.

Petition: Come, Holy Spirit...

SPIRIT OF JUDGMENT

Scripture: Isaiah 4:4

The Lord will wash away the filth of the women of Zion; he will cleanse the blood-stains from Jerusalem by a Spirit of Judgment and a Spirit of Fire.

Reflection: Sin merits judgment. Judgment for the rebellion of the whole human race was death (Romans 6:23). Our God so loved us that in Christ He himself took on the penalty of death on our behalf (2 Corinthians 5:21). Yet, we who have been spared this ultimate judgment still fall into sin. The God who loves us also purifies us (1 John 1:7) through judgment and fire. For the believer it is a judgment unto mercy because it frees us to be more like Jesus. As the Apostle says ''...it is time for judgment to begin with the family of God'' (Peter 4:17a).

Prayer: Lord Jesus, send the Spirit of Judgment upon me that I may be refined and freed from the stain of sin in order to be more effective in your service, for your judgment for me is a sign of your mercy.

Decision: This day I will live my life in the light of the Spirit's judgment and scrutiny, not hiding my sin but letting the Lord wash it away.

Petition: Come, Holy Spirit...

SPIRIT OF KNOWLEDGE

Scripture: Isaiah 11:2
*The Spirit of the Lord will rest on him -
the Spirit of wisdom and of understanding,
the Spirit of counsel and of power, the
Spirit of knowledge and of the fear of the
Lord.*

Reflection: Knowledge has been sought
after for ages by men and women
through their own efforts. Knowledge
has been elusive through the ages. Our
first parents sought its treasures (Genesis 2) and so left a legacy of error and
rebellion. Yet, peoples are destroyed
from lack of knowledge (Hosea 4:6).
True knowledge comes only from the
source of knowledge itself, the living
God. Only the Spirit of God can reveal
His mind (1 Corinthians 8:11). Knowledge is born in a believer who seeks
the Lord and "puts on the new self,
which is being renewed in the image
of its Creator" (Colossians 3:10).

Prayer: Father, you are the source of all
true knowledge and the Spirit of
Knowledge fully rests upon your perfect representation, Jesus. Teach me
this day to follow His path, the way

of the cross, and so be renewed in true knowledge.

Decision: Today I will destroy the altars of false knowledge I have surrounded myself with, and resolve to seek Him who is the beginning and the end of all knowledge.

Petition: Come, Holy Spirit...

SPIRIT OF LIFE

Scripture: Romans 8:1-2
Therefore, there is now no condemnation for those who are in Christ Jesus, because through Christ Jesus the law of the Spirit of life set me free from the law of sin and death.

Reflection: Jesus came to bring life (John 10:10) and His Spirit continues to bring life to all men and women who open their lives to His great gift. The burden and suffering of the human race are the fruit of sin (Romans 7:7). Rebellion against God's law brings as its wages death and bondage (Romans 6:23), but the gift of a loving God is eternal life in and through His Son (John 3:16). To those who are "hidden in Christ" (Colossians 3:3), the death sentence of sin has been executed through the Cross. The Spirit of Life is now poured out to bring freedom for the captives (Isaiah 61:1). We have victory even over death itself through the Author of Life (Hebrews 2:9).

Prayer: Lord Jesus Christ, I confess my own sin and rebellion and acknowledge the penalty my sin merits. Jesus,

I invite you into my life and accept the free gift of your atonement. Please fill me with the Spirit of Life. Free me from the effects of sin and death and make me a faithful disciple.

Decision: Today, I will throw off the chains of death my sin has merited and walk in the glorious freedom of Jesus Christ, filled with the Spirit of Life.

Petition: Come, Holy Spirit...

SPIRIT OF POWER

Scripture: Isaiah 11:2, Acts 1:8
*The Spirit of the Lord will rest on him -
the Spirit of wisdom and of understanding,
the Spirit of counsel and of power, the
Spirit of knowledge and of the fear of the
Lord.*

*. . . you will receive power when the Holy
Spirit comes upon you.*

Reflection: The Holy Spirit is a Spirit of
Power and that power is the
inheritance of those who follow the
anointed one, Jesus Christ. Jesus
promised to those who would wait in
Jerusalem that they would receive
power when the Holy Spirit came
upon them and they would be His witnesses (Act 1:8-9). The Greek word for
power is "dunamis", from which we
derive our word dynamite. The Holy
Spirit in the life of a believer is explo-
sive. We are no longer bound by the
timidity of our past lives but God has
given us "...a spirit of power, of love
and of self-discipline" (2 Timothy 1:7).

Prayer: Father, your Spirit of Power rested
upon Jesus your Son and on the day

47

of Pentecost you sent it upon His followers so that they could continue His mission. Give me more of that power so that I may demonstrate and proclaim that Jesus is Lord.

Decision: Today, I will walk in the power of the Holy Spirit and not be subject to the timidity and fear of my former way of living because the ''dynamite'' of the Spirit is within me.

Petition: Come, Holy Spirit...

SPIRIT OF PROPHECY

Scripture: Revelations 19:10

At this I fell at his feet to worship him. But he said to me, "Do not do it! I am a fellow servant with you and with your brothers who hold to the testimony of Jesus. Worship God! For the testimony of Jesus is the Spirit of Prophecy."

Reflection: "No one knows the mind of the Lord but the Spirit of the Lord..." (1 Corinthians 2:7) The spirit of the Lord is a prophetic spirit which reveals the purposes and plans of God Himself to both the church and the individual believer. When the spirit of Jesus is present within us we no longer remain in the dark, rather we commune with God and He speaks His mind to us. This should lead us to follow the command of the servant of the Lord to the apostle John, and "Worship God." We are children of the Light and our paths are filled with hope because by the spirit of God we no longer walk in futility but with purpose. We can know the Lord's word if we but wait on Him.

Prayer: Lord, fill me with the Holy Spirit that I might be a witness to Jesus and reveal your great plan for all men. Give me the gift of prophecy so that I might speak forth your words to a people who so desperately need to hear them.

Decision: Today I will wait on the Lord in my prayer and seek to hear His word in the recesses of my heart so that I can live it out in my daily life.

Petition: Come, Holy Spirit...

SPIRIT OF SONSHIP

Scripture: Romans 8:15

For you did not receive a spirit that makes you a slave again to fear, but you received the Spirit of Sonship. And by him we cry, "Abba, Father."

Reflection: To be a Son is to be included, included in the very life of God, part of the family of God. It is the Holy Spirit, the agent of change and conversion that not only moves us into the family but cleans us up to look like our Father. "Like Father, like Son," is a common saying, and so it is with all of us who have received Jesus.

Any who did accept Him, He empowered to become children of God. These are they who believe in his name - who were begotten not by blood, nor by carnal desire, nor by man's willing it, but by God" (John 1:12-13 NAB).

Prayer: Father, hear the prayers of your son/daughter this day as I make them through your beloved Son Jesus. Let your Spirit of Sonship confirm my place in the family and conform me

more to the image of your beloved
Son, Jesus.

Decision: Today I will live as a member
of the family of God.

Petition: Come, Holy Spirit...

SPIRIT OF THE FEAR OF THE LORD

Scripture: Isaiah 11:2

*The Spirit of the Lord will rest on him -
the Spirit of wisdom and of understanding,
the Spirit of counsel and of power, the
Spirit of knowledge and of the fear of the
Lord.*

Reflection: The Fear of the Lord is the
beginning of wisdom (Proverbs 9:10)
and knowledge (Proverbs 1:7). It adds
length to our life (Proverbs 10:27), is
a fountain of life (Proverbs 14:27) and
teaches us humility (Proverbs 15:33).
Fear, which the Holy Spirit inspires,
leads us to acknowledge God's awe-
some sovereignty and our puniness so
that we fall on our knees and worship
God. Unlike mere human fear, the
Spirit of the Fear of the Lord brings us
to the gate of true worship, enabling
us to see the majesty of God. This is
the worship the Father deserves, worship in Spirit and in truth (John 4:24).

Prayer: Father, you are an all-holy God
and I am steeped in sin. In Jesus I am
made new and fresh (2 Corinthians

5:17). Give me Lord a right Spirit of fear and reverence for your majesty that will lead me to worship and to a right posture before you. Grant me not a fear of punishment, for the perfect love demonstrated by your Son casts out that fear (1 John 4:7), but a fear of offending you my God who deserves my all in all.

Decision: Today I will seriously attempt to live my life in right fear before the living God and lead a life of worship.

Petition: Come, Holy Spirit...

SPIRIT OF THE SON

Scripture: Galatians 4:6

Because you are sons, God sent the spirit of His Son into our hearts, the spirit who calls out, "Abba, Father."

Reflection: No longer orphans! No longer alienated! Brought into the family of the living God! Our lives are now "hidden in Christ" (Colossians 3:3). By the working of the Holy Spirit we now stand in the same privileged relationship Jesus has with the Father, caught up in the very life of God. We stand in "His shoes" and can speak to God as "Abba," "Dad," with a holy reverence and personal affection. Also, we can begin to look more and more like the "firstborn," the older brother among many who would come after Him, born into the family by the Holy Spirit (Romans 8:29). We have the same status, the same inheritance, and now the same mission to bring a straying humanity back to the family.

Prayer: Father, Abba, give me the wisdom, courage, and grace I need to carry on the mission of the firstborn son so that I might present new sons and daughters to you this day, born into the family through the Holy Spirit.

Decision: Today I will live as a son/daughter of God and act as though He were indeed my Father.

Petition: Come, Holy Spirit...

SPIRIT OF THE SOVEREIGN LORD

Scripture: Isaiah 61:1

*The Spirit of the Sovereign Lord is on me,
because the Lord has anointed me to preach
good news to the poor. He has sent me to
bind up the brokenhearted, to proclaim freedom for the captives and release for the
prisoners...*

Reflection: When one lives under a sovereign, one lives completely subject to
His rule. Sovereignty is a democratic
and equalitarian approach to govern-
ment. Yet God is sovereign, ''...over
the kingdoms of men and gives them
to any one He wishes'' (Daniel 4:25).
It is a fact that God rules over all even
over those who do not acknowledge
Him. Sovereignty, in all its regal
authority, rested upon our Master,
Jesus Christ (Matthew 28:18). He
imparted that sovereignty on us as
ambassadors of a Sovereign (2 Corinthians 5:20), sent on a mission of
proclamation, reconciliation and
restoration.

Prayer: Father you placed your Spirit upon your Son Jesus and sent Him forth to establish your reign. Teach me this day to live under your sovereignty and extend your dominion to those around me through proclaiming and living the Good News.

Decision: Today I will live my life acknowledging the sovereignty of God and trusting that all things work together for His good and therefore for my own. I am the messenger of the King and I will herald His good news.

Petition: Come, Holy Spirit...

SPIRIT OF TRUTH

Scripture: John 16:13

But when he, the Spirit of Truth, comes, he will guide you into all truth. He will not speak on his own; He will speak only what he hears, and he will tell you what is yet to come.

Reflection: Pontius Pilate, in the presence of divinity, mockingly cried out "What is truth?" (St. John 18:38). He had become so blinded by the cares of this world and the deception of power that He did not even recognize its personification. Standing before him was the One who had proclaimed Himself, "the Way, the Truth and the Life" (St. John 14:6). In an age where so much competes for our affection and loyalty, the Lord wants to purify us by the truth. His Word alone is truth (John 17:17). We have not been left alone. The Spirit of the truth guides us and protects us from falsehood and deception.

Prayer: Lord, fill me with your Spirit of Truth. Purify me in truth. Root out any falsehood that I may hear your voice and know your way.

Decision: Today I will be open to purification by the Spirit of Truth so that I can follow in the footsteps of the one who is the Way, the Truth and the Life, Jesus Christ.

Petition: Come, Holy Spirit...

SPIRIT OF UNDERSTANDING

Scripture: Isaiah 11:2

The Spirit of the Lord will rest on him - the spirit of the wisdom and of understanding, the Spirit of counsel and of power, the Spirit of knowledge and of the fear of the Lord.

Reflection: Through the Prophet Isaiah, God promised the gift of understanding. In Christ Jesus, that and all the promises of God have been fulfilled. He is indeed the ''yes'' to all the promises of God (2 Corinthians 1:21). The Spirit of Understanding leads us into a relationship with the Lord where our minds are changed and renewed (Romans 12:2). We begin to understand by standing under God's word, His law and the direction of His church. It is in that relationship that we find true understanding.

Prayer: Lord, fill me with your Spirit of Understanding that my mind may be renewed and my life transformed by obedience to your word and your church.

Decision: Today, I will co-operate with the work of the Holy Spirit that I may "stand under" God's plan, His word and the direction of His church.

Petition: Come, Holy Spirit...

SPIRIT OF WISDOM

Scripture: Isaiah 11:2
> *The spirit of the Lord will rest on him - the Spirit of wisdom and of understanding, the Spirit of counsel and of power, the Spirit of knowledge and of the fear of the Lord.*

Reflection: It is the Lord who gives Wisdom (Proverbs 2:6) and fear of Him is its beginning (Proverbs 1:7). He often produces fruit in the life of His people through their voluntary humility (Proverbs 11:2); the rod of correction (Proverbs 29:15) and through His Holy Spirit which is the source and summit of Wisdom. The Spirit imparts a wisdom from above, not a worldly wisdom which is futile and foolish (1 Corinthians 3:19-20). His Spirit of Wisdom is given generously to all who ask (James 1:15).

Prayer: God of infinite Wisdom give me more of your Spirit of Wisdom that I might judge rightly and live righteously before you.

Decision: Today I will rely less on human wisdom and more on divine wisdom, seeking the aid of the Spirit of Wisdom.

Petition: Come, Holy Spirit...

WILLING SPIRIT

Scripture: Psalm 51:12

Do not cast me from your presence or take your Holy Spirit from me, restore to me the joy of your salvation and grant me a willing spirit, to sustain me.

Reflection: The Holy Spirit is a willing and submissive spirit as demonstrated by the perfect submission of Jesus, who laid aside His claims to equality with God and took the form of a servant (Philippians 2). It was through this Willing Spirit that He accomplished the greatest act of love in human history and ended the long reign of sin and darkness. This Willing Spirit should characterize and animate those who follow after Him and continue His mission. This was His direction on that solemn night when He rose from the table and washed the disciples' feet (John 13). He instructed them to do as He had done. This was the heart cry of the Master in that Garden when He fought through His own agony and human travail and cried out to His Father, "Not My will but Yours be done" (Matthew 26:39). This mandate is reiterated in the admonition of St. Paul, ''Have this attitude in you which was in Christ Jesus'' (Philippians 2). We need to conform our human wills to the will of the Father and demonstrate that we are indeed filled with the Holy Spirit, the Willing Spirit that possesses the servants of the Most High.

Prayer: Father fill me with the Willing Spirit that motivated Jesus, your Perfect Servant, so that I may always be willing to prefer your purposes over my own plans and desires.

Decision: Today I will conform my human will to the divine will, through the power of the Willing Spirit within me.

Petition: Come, Holy Spirit. . .

PART II
Prayers to the Holy Spirit

INVOCATION TO THE HOLY SPIRIT

V. Come, Holy Spirit, fill the hearts of your faithful and kindle in them the fire of your divine love.

R. Send forth your Spirit and they shall be created: And you will renew the face of the earth.

Let us pray: O God, who by the light of the Holy Spirit instructs the hearts of the faithful, grant we beseech you to be truly wise and ever rejoice in His presence, through Jesus Christ Our Lord. Amen.

PRAYER TO THE HOLY SPIRIT

O Holy Spirit, soul of my soul,
I adore You.
Enlighten, guide, strengthen, and console me.
Tell me what I ought to do and command Me to do it.
I promise to be submissive in everything You permit to happen to me;
Only show me what is Your will!

(Cardinal Mercier)

PRAYER OF POPE JOHN FOR THE SECOND VATICAN COUNCIL

Renew in our own days your miracles as of a second Pentecost.

O divine Spirit, sent by the Father in the name of Jesus, give your aid and infallible guidance to your Church and pour out on the Ecumenical Council the fullness of your gifts.

O gentle Teacher and Consoler, enlighten the hearts of our prelates who, eagerly responding to the call of the Supreme Roman Pontiff, will gather here in solemn conclave.

May this Council produce abundant fruits; may the light and power of the gospel be more widely diffused in human society; may new vigor be imparted to the Catholic religion and its missionary function; may we all acquire a more profound knowledge of the Church's doctrine and a wholesome increase of Christian morality.

O gentle Guest of our souls, confirm our minds in truth and dispose our hearts to obedience, that the deliberations of the

Council may find in us generous consent and prompt obedience.

We pray to you again for the lambs who are no longer part of the one fold of Jesus Christ, that they too, who still glory in the name of Christians, may at last be united under one shepherd.

Renew in our own days your miracles as of a second Pentecost; and grant that Holy Church, reunited in one prayer, more fervent than before, around Mary, the mother of Jesus, and under the leadership of Peter, may extend the kingdom of truth, justice, love and peace. Amen.

CONSECRATION TO
THE HOLY SPIRIT

On my knees before
the great cloud of witnesses,
I offer myself soul and body to You,
Eternal Spirit of God.
I adore the brightness of Your purity,
The unerring keenness of Your justice,
And the might of Your love.
You are the strength and the light of my
    soul;
In You I live and move and am;
I desire never to grieve You by
    unfaithfulness
To grace, and I pray with all my heart
To be kept from the smallest sin against
    You.
Make me faithful in every thought,
And grant that I may always listen to Your
    voice,
Watch for Your light, and follow Your
    gracious inspiration.
I cling to You and give myself to You
And ask You by Your compassion
To watch over me in my weakness.
Holding the pierced feet of Jesus,
And looking at His five wounds,
And trusting to His precious blood,

And adoring His opened side and stricken
heart,
I implore You, Adorable Spirit,
Helper of my infirmity, so to keep me
In Your grace that I may never sin against
You
With the sin which You cannot forgive.

Give me grace, O Holy Ghost,
Spirit of the Father and the Son,
To say to You always and everywhere,
"Speak, Lord, for Your servant is
listening."

O Spirit of Wisdom, preside over all my
thoughts,
Words, and actions, from this hour
Till the moment of my death.

Spirit of Understanding, enlighten and
teach me.
Spirit of Counsel, direct my inexperience.
Spirit of Fortitude, strengthen my
weakness.
Spirit of Knowledge, instruct my
ignorance.
Spirit of Piety, make me fervent in good
works.
Spirit of Fear, restrain me from all evil.
Spirit of Peace, give me Your peace.

Heavenly Spirit, make me persevere in the
service of God,
And enable me to act on all occasions with
goodness and benignity,
Patience, charity, and joy, longanimity,
mildness and fidelity.
Let the heavenly virtues of modesty,
continency, and chastity adorn the temple
You have chosen for Your abode.
O Spirit of Holiness,
By Your all-powerful grace, preserve my
soul from the misfortune of sin. Amen.

OFFICE OF THE
HOLY SPIRIT

MATINS

V. The grace of the Holy Spirit illuminate our senses and hearts.

R. Amen.

V. O Lord, You will open my lips,

R. And my mouth shall declare Your praise.

V. Incline unto my aid, O God.

R. O Lord, make haste to help me.

V. Glory be to the Father and to the Son and to the Holy Spirit.

R. As it was in the beginning, is now, and ever shall be, world without end. Amen.

Hymn

The Holy Spirit our souls invest
With grace that does o'ershade the best
Of virgin maids, when from the spheres
An Angel came to greet her ears;
The Word Divine did flesh become,
And fruitful made a virgin womb.

Ant. Come, Holy Spirit, fill the hearts of Your faithful, and kindle in them the fire of Your love.

V. Send forth Your Spirit, and they shall be created.

R. And You shall renew the face of the earth.

Prayer

We beseech You, O Lord, that the virtue of Your Holy Spirit may be present with us, which may both purify our hearts and defend us from all adversities; through our Lord Jesus Christ, Your Son, who with You and the same Holy Spirit, lives and reigns. Amen.

PRIME

V. The grace of the Holy Spirit, etc.

Hymn

Christ, born of Mary, that blest maid,
Was crucified, was dead, was laid
Within a tomb, from whence He rose,
And did His person soon disclose
To His disciples, in whose sight
He soared above the starry height.

(The antiphon, verse, response, and prayer as before)

TERCE

V. The grace of the Holy Spirit, etc.

Hymn

God sent from heaven the Holy Spirit
Upon the day of Pentecost;
He did the Apostles' minds inspire,
Inflaming them with tongues of fire;
He would not have them orphans left,
When of the sight of Christ bereft.
(The antiphon, verse, response, and
  prayer as before)

SEXT

V. The grace of the Holy Spirit, etc.

Hymn

With sevenfold grace God did enrich
The Apostles, then by means of which
They did both speak and understand
The language of each distant land:
To preach Christ's faith, they then
  dispersed
Themselves throughout the universe.
(The antiphon, verse, response, and
  prayer as before)

NONE

V. The grace of the Holy Spirit, etc.

Hymn

The consoling Spirit He
Entitled was, true charity;
The gift of God; a fire inflamed;
The vivifying fountain named;
A spiritual unction; sevenfold grace;
A free gift of celestial race.
(The antiphon, verse, response, and
  prayer as before)

VESPERS

V. The grace of the Holy Spirit, etc.

Hymn

The right hand finger of our Lord,
His spiritual power to us afford
A safe defense against all evil,
That harmed we be not by the devil.
Protect us, nourish us, and bring
Us under shelter of Your wing.
(The antiphon, verse, response, and
  prayer as before)

COMPLINE

V. The grace of the Holy Spirit, etc.

V. Convert us, O God, our Saviour.
R. And avert Your anger from us.
V. Incline unto our aid, O God.
R. O Lord, make haste to help us.
V. Glory be to the Father, etc.

Hymn

Vouchsafe, O holy Paraclete,
To pour into our souls Your light,
And to direct us in our ways,
That when to judgment God shall raise
The sleeping world, He bid us stand
Upon His right and saving hand.
(The antiphon, verse, response, and
  prayer as before)

COMMENDATION

These hours canonical to You,
O Holy Spirit, addressed be,
With piously devoted hearts;
That to our souls You may impart
Your inspirations, and that we
May live in heaven eternally. Amen.

LITANY TO THE SPIRIT

Come, Spirit of Wisdom, and teach us to
value the highest gift.
Come Holy Spirit.

Come, Spirit of Understanding, and show
us all things in the light of eternity.
Come Holy Spirit.

Come, Spirit of Counsel, and guide us
along the straight and narrow path
to our heavenly home.
Come Holy Spirit.

Come, Spirit of Might, and strengthen us
against every evil spirit and
interest which would separate us
from you.
Come Holy Spirit.

Come, Spirit of Knowledge, and teach us
the shortness of life and the length
of eternity.
Come Holy Spirit.

Come, Spirit of Godliness, and stir up our
minds and hearts to love and serve
the Lord our God all our days.
Come Holy Spirit.

Come, Spirit of the Fear of the Lord, and
make us tremble with awe and
reverence before your divine
majesty.
Come Holy Spirit.

NOVENA TO THE HOLY SPIRIT

The novena in honor of the Holy Spirit is the oldest of all novenas since it was first made at the direction of our Lord Himself when He sent His apostles back to Jerusalem to await the coming of the Holy Spirit on the first Pentecost. It is still the only novena officially prescribed by the Church. Addressed to the Third Person of the Blessed Trinity, it is a powerful plea for the light and strength and love so sorely needed by every Christian. To encourage devotion to the Holy Spirit, the Church has enriched this novena with indulgences.

ACT OF CONSECRATION TO THE HOLY SPIRIT

On my knees before the great multitude of heavenly witness, I offer myself, soul and body to You, Eternal Spirit of God. I adore the brightness of Your purity, the unerring keenness of Your justice, and the might of Your love. You are the strength and the light of my soul. In You I live and move and am. I desire never to grieve You by unfaithfulness to grace, and I pray with all my heart to be kept from the smallest sin against You. Mercifully guard my every thought and grant that I may always watch for Your light and listen to Your voice and follow Your gracious inspirations. I cling to You, and give myself to You, and ask You by Your compassion to watch over me in my weakness. Holding the pierced Feet of Jesus and looking at His Five Wounds and trusting in His Precious Blood and adoring His opened Side and stricken Heart, I implore You, Adorable Spirit, Helper of my infirmity, so to keep me in Your grace that I may never sin against You. Give me grace, O Holy Spirit, Spirit of the Father and the Son to say to

you always and everywhere "Speak Lord for Your servant heareth." Amen.
(To be recited daily during the Novena)

PRAYER FOR THE
SEVEN GIFTS OF THE
HOLY SPIRIT

O Lord Jesus Christ Who,
Before ascending into heaven
Promised to send the Holy Spirit
To finish your work
In the souls of Your Apostles and Disciples.
Grant that same Holy Spirit to me,
That He may perfect in my soul
The work of Your grace and Your love.
Grant me:
The Spirit of Wisdom
  That I may despise
  The perishable things of this world
  And aspire only after
  The things that are eternal,
The Spirit of Understanding
  To enlighten my mind
  With the light of Your divine truth,
The Spirit of Counsel
  That I may ever choose
  The surest way of pleasing God
  And gaining heaven,
The Spirit of Fortitude
  That I may bear my cross with You
  And that I may overcome with courage
  All the obstacles
  That oppose my salvation,

The Spirit of Knowledge
   That I may know God
   And know myself and
   Grow perfect in the science of the Saints,
The Spirit of Piety
   That I may find
   The service of God sweet and amiable,
The Spirit of Fear
   That I may be filled
   With a loving reverence towards God
   And may dread in any way to displease
      Him.
Mark me, dear Lord,
With the sign of Your true disciples and
Animate me in all things with Your Spirit.
   Amen.
(To be recited daily during the Novena)

FIRST DAY

Holy Spirit! Lord of light!
From Your clear celestial height,
Your pure beaming radiance give!

The Holy Spirit

Only one thing is important - eternal salvation. Only one thing, therefore, is to be feared - sin. Sin is the result of ignorance, weakness, and indifference. The Holy Spirit is the Spirit of Light, of Strength, and of Love. With His sevenfold gifts He enlightens the mind, strengthens the will, and inflames the heart with love of God. To ensure our salvation, we ought to invoke the Divine Spirit daily, for ''The Spirit helps in our infirmity. We know not what we should pray for as we ought. But the Spirit Himself asks for us.''

Prayer

Almighty and eternal God, Who has vouchsafed to regenerate us by water and the Holy Spirit, and has given us forgiveness of all sins, vouchsafe to send forth from heaven upon us Your sevenfold Spirit, the Spirit of Wisdom and Understanding, the Spirit of Counsel and Fortitude, the Spirit of Knowledge and Piety, and fill us with the Spirit of Holy Fear. Amen.

Our Father and Hail Mary ONCE.
Glory be to the Father SEVEN TIMES.
Act of Consecration, Prayer for the Seven Gifts.

SECOND DAY

Come, Father of the poor!
Come, treasures which endure!
Come, Light of all that live!

The Gift of Fear

The gift of Fear fills us with a sovereign respect for God, and makes us dread nothing so much as to offend Him by sin. It is a fear that arises, not from the thought of hell, but from sentiments of reverence and filial submission to our heavenly Father. It is this fear that is the beginning of wisdom, detaching us from worldly pleasures that could in any way separate us from God. ''They that fear the Lord will prepare their hearts, and in His sight will sanctify their souls.''

Prayer

Come, O blessed Spirit of Holy Fear, penetrate my inmost heart, that I may set

You, my Lord and God, before my face forever; help me to shun all things that can offend You, and make me worthy to appear before the pure eyes of Your Divine Majesty in heaven, where You live and reign in the unity of the ever Blessed Trinity, God, world without end. Amen.

Our Father and Hail Mary ONCE.
Glory be to the Father SEVEN TIMES.
Act of Consecration, Prayer for the Seven Gifts.

THIRD DAY

Thou, of all consolers best,
Visiting the troubled breast,
Dost refreshing peace bestow.

The Gift of Piety

The gift of Piety begets in our hearts a filial affection for God as our most loving Father. It inspires us to love and respect, for His sake, persons and things consecrated to Him, as well as those who are vested with His authority, His Blessed Mother and the Saints, the Church and its visible Head, our parents and superiors, our country and its rulers. He who is filled with the gift of Piety finds the practice of his religion not a burdensome duty, but a delightful service. Where there is love, there is no labor.

Prayer

Come, O Blessed Spirit of Piety, possess my heart. Enkindle in me such a love for God, that I may find satisfaction only in His service, and for His sake lovingly submit to all legitimate authority. Amen.

Our Father and Hail Mary ONCE.
Glory be to the Father SEVEN TIMES.
Act of Consecration, Prayer for the Seven Gifts.

FOURTH DAY

Thou in toil art comfort sweet;
Pleasant coolness in the heat;
Solace in the midst of woe.

The Gift of Fortitude

By the gift of Fortitude the soul is strengthened against natural fear, and supported to the end in the performance of duty. Fortitude imparts to the will an impulse and energy which move it to undertake without hesitancy the most arduous tasks, to face dangers, to trample under foot human respect, and to endure without complaint the slow martyrdom of even lifelong tribulation. "He that shall persevere unto the end, he shall be saved."

Prayer

Come, O Blessed Spirit of Fortitude, uphold my soul in time of trouble and adversity, sustain my efforts after holiness, strengthen my weakness, give me courage against all the assaults of my enemies, that I may never be overcome and separated from You, my God and greatest Good. Amen.

Our Father and Hail Mary ONCE.
Glory be to the Father SEVEN TIMES.
Act of Consecration, Prayer for the Seven Gifts.

FIFTH DAY

Light immortal! Light Divine!
Visit Thou these hearts of Thine,
And our inmost being fill!

The Gift of Knowledge

The gift of Knowledge enables the soul to evaluate created things at their true worth - in their relation to God. Knowledge unmasks the pretense of creatures, reveals their emptiness, and points out their only true purpose as instruments in the service of God. It shows us the loving care of God even in adversity, and directs us to glorify Him in every circumstance of life. Guided by its light, we put first things first, and prize the friendship of God beyond all else. ''Knowledge is a fountain of life to him that possesses it.''

Prayer

Come, O Blessed Spirit of Knowledge, and grant that I may perceive the will of the Father; show me the nothingness of earthly things, that I may realize their vanity and use them only for Your glory and my own salvation, looking ever beyond them to You, and Your eternal rewards. Amen.

Our Father and Hail Mary ONCE.
Glory be to the Father SEVEN TIMES.
Act of Consecration, Prayer for the Seven Gifts.

SIXTH DAY

If Thou take Thy grace away,
Nothing pure in man will stay,
All his good is turned to ill.

The Gift of Understanding

Understanding, as a gift of the Holy Spirit, helps us to grasp the meaning of the truths of our holy religion. By faith we know them, but by Understanding we learn to appreciate and relish them. It enables us to penetrate the inner meaning of revealed truths and through them to be quickened to newness of life. Our faith ceases to be sterile and inactive, but inspires a mode of life that bears eloquent testimony to the faith that is in us; we begin to ''walk worthy of God in all things pleasing, and increasing in the knowledge of God.''

Prayer

Come, O Spirit of Understanding, and enlighten our minds, that we may know and believe all the mysteries of salvation; and may merit at last to see the eternal light in Your Light; and in the light of glory to have a clear vision of You and the Father and the Son. Amen.

Our Father and Hail Mary ONCE.
Glory be to the Father SEVEN TIMES.
Act of Consecration, Prayer for the Seven Gifts.

SEVENTH DAY

Heal our wounds - our strength renew;
On our dryness pour Thy dew;
Wash the stains of guilt away!

The Gift of Counsel

The gift of Counsel endows the soul with supernatural prudence, enabling it to judge promptly and rightly what must be done, especially in difficult circumstances. Counsel applies in the principles furnished by Knowledge and Understanding to the innumerable concrete cases that confront us in the course of our daily duty as parents, teachers, public servants, and Christian citizens. Counsel is supernatural common sense, a priceless treasure in the quest of salvation. "Above all these things, pray to the Most High, that He may direct Your way in truth."

Prayer

Come, O Spirit of Counsel, help and guide me in all my ways, that I may always do Your holy will. Incline my heart to that which is good; turn it away from all that is evil, and direct me by the straight path of Your commandments to that goal of eternal life for which I long. Amen.

Our Father and Hail Mary ONCE.
Glory be to the Father SEVEN TIMES.
Act of Consecration, Prayer for the Seven Gifts.

EIGHTH DAY

Bend the stubborn heart and will;
Melt the frozen warm the chill;
Guide the steps that go astray!

The Gift of Wisdom

Embodying all the other gifts, as charity embraces all the other virtues, Wisdom is the most perfect of the gifts. Of wisdom it is written "all good things come to me with her, and innumerable riches through her hands." It is the gift of Wisdom that strengthens our faith, fortifies hope, perfects charity, and promotes the practice of virtue in the highest degree. Wisdom enlightens the mind to discern and relish things divine, in the appreciation of which earthly joys lose their savor, while the Cross of Christ yields a divine sweetness according to the words of the Saviour: "Take up the cross and follow me, for my yoke is sweet and my burden light."

Prayer

Come, O Spirit of Wisdom, and reveal to my soul the mysteries of heavenly things, their exceeding greatness, power and beauty. Teach me to love them above and beyond all the passing joys and satis-

factions of earth. Help me to attain them
and possess them for ever. Amen.

Our Father and Hail Mary ONCE.
Glory be to the Father SEVEN TIMES.
Act of Consecration, Prayer for the Seven Gifts.

NINTH DAY

Thou, on those who evermore
Thee confess and Thee adore,
In Thy sevenfold gifts, descend;
Give them comfort when they die;
Give them life with Thee on high;
Give them joys which never end. Amen.

The Fruits of the Holy Spirit

The gifts of the Holy Spirit perfect the
supernatural virtues by enabling us to
practice them with greater docility to
divine inspiration. As we grow in the
knowledge and love of God under the
direction of the Holy Spirit, our service
becomes more sincere and generous, the
practice of virtue, more perfect. Such acts
of virtue leave the heart filled with joy and
consolation and are known as Fruits of the
Holy Spirit. These Fruits in turn render the
practice of virtue more attractive and
become a powerful incentive for still

greater efforts in the service of God, to serve Whom is to reign.

Prayer

Come, O Divine Spirit, fill my heart with Your heavenly fruits, Your charity, joy, peace, patience, benignity, goodness, faith, mildness, and temperance, that I may never weary in the service of God, but by continued faithful submission to Your inspiration may merit to be united eternally with You in the love of the Father and the Son. Amen.

Our Father and Hail Mary ONCE.
Glory be to the Father SEVEN TIMES.
Act of Consecration, Prayer for the Seven Gifts.